MW01139796

DIVERSITY to me

LA DIVERSIDAD PARA MÍ

By Marisa J. Taylor

Illustrated By Fernanda Monteiro

BILINGUAL
English - Spanish

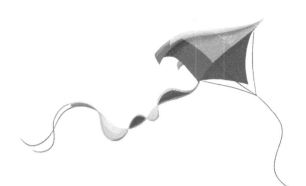

LINGO
BABIES

Diversity To Me
La Diversidad Para Mí

Text & Illustration Copyright © 2022 by Lingobabies

Written by Marisa Taylor
Illustrated by Fernanda Monteiro

ISBN: 978-1-914605-18-5 (paperback)
ISBN: 978-1-914605-19-2 (hardcover)

Edited by Shari Black
Spanish Translation by Gabriella Aldeman
Graphic Design edits by Clementina Cortés

DEDICATION

This book is dedicated to all the children of the world who feel insecure about their differences. May you learn to love and embrace what makes you different from the rest.

Every day tell yourself one thing you love about yourself and always remember that you are perfect just the way you are.

This book is also dedicated to my children, who I love dearly. You inspire me to be a better person and to use my voice to stand up against racism & inequalities.

Este libro está dedicado a todos los niños que se sienten inseguros acerca de sus diferencias.

Que aprendas a amar y abrazar lo que te hace ser diferente del resto. Cada día mírate en el espejo y di una cosa que amas de ti y recuerda siempre que eres perfecto tal como eres.

Este libro también está dedicado a mis hijas, a quienes amo mucho. Me inspiran a ser una mejor persona y a usar mi voz para luchar contra el racismo.

Marisa Taylor

Hi, what's your name?

¿Hola, cómo te llamas?

....

Hi,
my name is Havana.

Hola,
me llamo Havana.

Do you know the word "diversity"?
Let me tell you what that word means to me.

¿Conoces la palabra «diversidad»?
Te digo lo que significa para mí,
si me das la oportunidad.

Diversity is about being different:
A different look, a different culture, a different race.
A different ethnicity - even a different face.

La diversidad se trata
de ser diferente:
Distintas culturas,
razas y gente.
Es tener un aspecto único,
una cara diferente.

Everyone is born different,
and that is a wonderful thing.

Todos nacimos distintos;
todos somos originales.

**Because if everyone was born the same,
the world would be boring.**

Pues qué aburrido sería el mundo,
si todos fuéramos iguales.

I love the word "different".
It makes me feel free.
It reminds me that
no one is the same.
There is only one me.

Me encanta la palabra «diferente».
Me da un sentimiento de libertad.
Me recuerda que nadie es igual y
yo soy única en la humanidad.

I have curly hair, brown skin,
and freckles on my face.
But that's not what defines me.
It's my joy and style and grace.

Yo tengo el cabello rizado,
piel morena y pecas en la nariz.
Pero eso no es todo lo que me define.
También tengo mi propia gracia
y estilo, y así soy feliz.

My friend Ore is different,
too: he is not like me.
He is shy and quiet - the
kindest kid you'll ever see.

Mi amigo Ore no es como yo:
él es diferente también.
Es tímido, tranquilo y amable,
y así cae a todos muy bien.

Alexia is different, too.
She loves to paint and run.
She's the fastest kid I know.
Together we have such fun!

Alexia también es diferente.
Le encanta correr y pintar.
Es la más rápida de todos.
¡Con ella me encanta jugar!

My friend Noah is an artist - he's
definitely unique.
He's also such a joker,
I laugh each time we speak.

Mi amigo Noah es un artista,
definitivamente singular.
También es muy chistoso:
me hace reír sin parar.

We all are beautiful!
We have special powers to offer the world,
and that is our story.

Todos somos hermosos,
con poderes diferentes que ofrecer.

We should never judge
someone for who they are,
but accept them in all their glory.

Por eso no debemos juzgar
a nadie, sino aceptarlos
sin ofender.

Our physical, cultural, and religious differences make the world a beautiful place.

Nuestras diferencias físicas,
culturales y religiosas
hacen del mundo
un lugar precioso.

BUS STOP

001
DIV

Differences are beautiful,
and are there for us to embrace.

Así que hay que aceptar nuestras diferencias
para que todo sea maravilloso.

Everyone has their own special talents. That's what makes us shine - you and me.
And that is the true beauty of diversity.

Todos tenemos talentos especiales
que nos hacen brillar de verdad.
Y esa es la importancia
y belleza de esta palabra:
diversidad.

DIVERSITY

What does diversity mean to you?

¿Qué significa la diversidad para ti?

About the creators

Marisa Taylor is a German/Canadian Author who resides in London, UK with her husband and children. They are a multiracial & multilingual family. Marisa has always been interested in learning & teaching languages, as she feels that it is the key element to connecting with people from other cultures. After becoming a mother she saw the lack of diverse resources available and became passionate about creating diverse bilingual resources that encourage children to celebrate multiculturalism and to learn a second language.

Instagram: @lingobabies

Fernanda Monteiro is a Brazilian illustrator and a mother of two, Íris and Aurora. She graduated in journalism, but her dream was always to work with drawing and found that the best way to do this would be through creating illustrations for children's books. Fernanda believes that through art she can contribute towards a better world in the future.

Instagram: @fe.monteiro_art

Otros libros bilingües

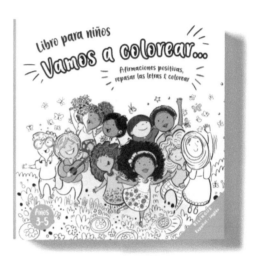

www.lingobabies.com